TRADITIONS OF
BREAD AND
VIOLENCE

TRADITIONS OF BREAD AND VIOLENCE

Poems by

CATHERINE SASANOV

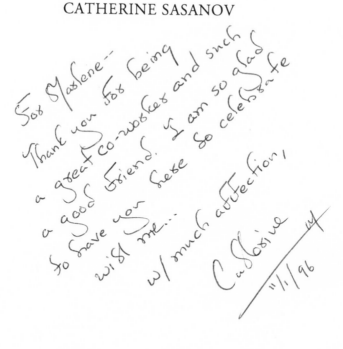

For Marlene--
Thank you for being
a great co-worker and such
a good friend. I am so glad
to have you here so celebrate
with me...
w/ much affection!
C Sasanov
11/1/96

FOUR WAY BOOKS

Marshfield

Editorial Office
Four Way Books
PO Box 607
Marshfield, MA 02050

Library of Congress Catalog Card Number : 95-61373

ISBN 1-884800-09-2

Cover design by Zuzzolo Graphics, Inc.
Cover art: "La Mano Poderosa." Anonymous artist.
19th century, Mexico. Collection of the author.
Text design by Acme Art, Inc.

Manufactured in the United States of America

This book is printed on acid-free paper.

Four Way Books is a division of Friends of Writers, Inc.,
a Vermont-based not-for-profit organization.

For Paul

ACKNOWLEDGEMENTS

ACM (*Another Chicago Magazine*): "Recognizing Little Tortures"

Agni: "Excitement, The Need for"

Caliban: "Vellum," "Receiving the Violently Killed," "Vertical City" and "Illegals"

Chariton Review: "The American in Brazil Watches a French Film (Subtitles in English)"

Columbia: A Magazine of Poetry and Prose: "Scarecrow" (originally "Demolitions V")

Connecticut Poetry Review: "Crime"

The Fiddlehead: "Notes on Our Future Disinterment" and "All Hallows"

Fine Madness: "Salvage," "Fire/The Love of Objects," "Triptych of the Heart," "Heaven," "Ashes," "The Floor Plan," "Test" and "Recognition in Time of Evolution"

Graham House Review: "Exvotos: Michoacan, Mexico" and "Exvotos: El Señor de los Milagros Church, Mexico"

Hayden's Ferry Review: "Excavations: The Pigs of Gadara/The Bones in a Wall"

Kansas Quarterly Review: "All Hallows"

The Little Magazine: "Traditions of Bread and Violence," "The Mother Next Door to the Murderer's House" and "History"

The Malahat Review: "Demolitions III" (originally "Demolitions I"), "Demolitions I" (originally "Demolitions III"), "Demolitions II" and "Leaving the Emergency Room"

Mid-American Review: "Among the Disintegrating Angels," "Cathedral," "Opening the Border" and "Sugar Bones, Sugar Tears: Oaxaca, Mexico"

River Styx: "News" (originally "Demolitions IV") and "Skeleton Tableau"

Sonora Review: "When We Absorb Sound"

Some of these poems also appeared in the following chapbooks and anthology: *Signatures Poetry Pamphlet No. 8* (Dolphin Moon Press, 1987); *Demolitions* (La Calavera Press, 1993); and *The Four Way Reader # 1* (Four Way Books, 1996).

I would like to thank the MacDowell Colony, the Massachusetts Artists Foundation, the Massachusetts Cultural Council, and the New England Foundation for the Arts for their support in the completion of this manuscript.

With deep gratitude to my parents, John Knox and Margaret Sheehe Baker, for their love and understanding; to Gary Duehr and Gloria Mindock for their years of friendship, ruthless editing, and unswerving support; and, finally, in memory of Harold Grosowsky who never doubted this book would come into being.

TABLE OF CONTENTS

III.

When you work with knives, it's good to praise God.

Osvaldo Sanchez
En el Nombre del Padre

PART ONE

The American in Brazil
Watches a French Film
(Subtitles in English)

What is he saying
over the white dress
of his lover?

Against the restaurant,
the hands, their last night together,
I understood everything,

but this woman won't backdrop
to any translation.
Look how my language

drowns out in her dress.
Unbutton that blouse —
The movement of English

against her breasts
would raise the nipples before
her lover's hand slips

between flesh and the word.
On leaving this theater,
nothing I wear will absorb

the pale interpretation
that others drag daily
across me. My nerves are rubbed raw,

my clothes wear out.
I smell like the language
I've brought on myself.

Long Enough in Brazil
to Be at Home on the Scenic Side
of Its Postcards

Living here left me part
of the stiff view, backing up
not choicer words
just smaller print. Then the thousand words
a postcard already fronts with.

"São Paulo" makes it 1,002.

Deeper than the ink-change of status
(no more *turista*) is how
I don't think before I speak
anymore in the language.

Tickets, photos, English —
My homesickness is no longer
tempted by paper products. New York,

your export of trash
is rebuilt, shipped back as
empty boxes from this third world.

My possessions will not be in them.

News

There's no remounting
the landscape
for correspondence —

This confused country
is no postcard.
Its cities scatter

at the feet
of censors, location
razor-bladed out of

letter after letter —
sad confetti without context
waiting to ticker tape a war's end.

Who can we trust?
Each night in America,
the man paid to announce

our sorrow
is a man who obliterates
his birthplace from his voice.

Scarecrow

Lay your head on my chest.

Estimate
the number of heartbeats
in each collapsed house.

Which closets
burst apart by wind
made this series of men

knee-deep in corn
and dressed in rags?
Gather them back

as a room around us —
Both sides of board
knowing rain, guarding

against every small hunger
dropping out of the sky.
Inside, they are a shrine

already gone up:
A wall tormented with nails,
a face
covering that pain.

Exvotos:
Michoacan, Mexico

Here, mythology's so fragile
it's reinforced
with metal: leaded saints

in stained windows,
the national hero
pumped full of bullets.

Divine intervention
repeats itself on sheets
of tin — Is the chapel wall

a gallery of miracles
or close calls? Lord,
give me one

small disaster to escape from.
I want to feel
testimony beneath my feet,

see the saint
hovered over my head.
Don't abandon me

again at the edge
of a volcano filled with flowers,
while Mexico's government

calculates the maximum
hours of sunlight
into my days.

Exvotos:
El Señor de los Milagros Church

These miracles adhere
to tin;
posed against cold metal,

I'm flesh
in a vacation photo.
Sugar bones

melt on my tongue,
my lover bites
into a skull

personalized with his name.
When he dies
will signing the cross

sew my broken heart
shut? Silver arm,
silver crutch — Here,

each cured infirmity's
a charm pinned
to Christ's sacred heart.

But what prayers reach heaven
in a sky filled
with satellites? Each wish

deflected from God
breaks simultaneously
onto every tv.

Milagros:
San Cristobel de las Casas Church

As tourists
300,000 beds await us —
I want to be only flesh

tonight. In this church,
each part of my body's
hammered into metal,

then hung on a silken thread.
It's no murder
to hang dismembered

among faceless angels, tiny
locks and keys,
corn, cows,

revolvers — Each charm
a miracle
of tin, brass, silver.

Will God answer a need
not available in metal?
Let Him see

the dangerous crowding
on altars — Who pinned
the revolver

near the disembodied hand?
The brass locust
by the silver ear of corn?

Sugar Bones,
Sugar Tears: Oaxaca, Mexico

I pick tears off the bread and eat them.

I want to thank the baker
who cried on each loaf,
who ices names
on the foreheads of skulls.

For weeks I've lived
on his bones, tears.
I popped sweet skulls in my mouth,

swallowed
my dead lover's name
over and over: *Harold*

come back, Harold
it's your turn to eat.
Today for the dead

every table's an altar
where a glass of water's
set down
to attract what is good.

Let your ashes
drift over the border,
to this town with a name like a sob.
To have died is no sin here.

I'm waiting for you
on the Plaza of Scribes: Typists
type on stone benches
while the illiterate whisper

words of love in their ears.
Anonymous letters from women
who've eaten their names,
then the names of their loved ones,
all their lives.

Receiving the Violently Killed

Police lifted you out of your aura —
You left behind the education
clapped out of a pair
of erasers, a child's game

abandoned on a sidewalk.

The gold had been stripped
from your fingers, torn
from your neck.
But you were no saint. You made

short use of the dreamless sleep
I paid a mortician
to work into your face. The calm
rotting off your skull,

no surrender in
your bones: a white that you carry
only as a weapon — God says

I can't ask you back in the house for two years.
For now,
you can only be lawn
I can walk across.

How can God blame the violently killed
if their bones don't rise
docile from their bodies
to be sugared?

The back of your skull's
an ancient map of the moon:
Sea of Darkness,
Sea of Tranquility,
Marsh of Corruption.

Among the Disintegrating Angels

They descend bearing stones,
falling with the weight of a cathedral
on their backs.

After hundreds of years
near the ceiling,
they should have come down over us
like snow:

angels scattering like
a flock of birds,
shadowing our every move.
Guardian, where do you

fit into this scene?
Crawling over the rubble of heaven,
two women
haul their God off the dead.

The heart of Jesus
softened by blood
breaks in a hundred pieces —

mortal, mortal love.

Every stone turned over
bears a fragment of saint, wing,
cloud, sky.

Heaven embedded in flesh.
Heaven leaving each body

unrecognizable.

The Floor Plan

Christ rose from his cross,
left me
at an intersection with four dead ends.

*

In dark rooms,
any screen in a thin wall
offers the possibility of forgiveness,
but sin permeates the booth
I kneel down in
over and over again.

*

Once I lived in a city large enough
to drown
the stars out of the sky
with its light;
its cathedral dismantled
stone by stone, dragged off
to become a village —
Are those who live there more blessed?

*

I'm hungry
and the only recipe in this house
is for the Lord's flesh —
It takes 15 minutes
to dissolve God
inside me.

*

I've made his heaven
my obstacle course: Prayers
tear on the points of each star,
till not even God can decipher
my desire.

Triptych of the Heart

I.

It's Jesus
standing at the side of the road,
heart in his hand.
His heart is a burr; it snags
on everything.
All thorns and fire: the love
fenced off and burning.

He's scared it will fall back
into his body; in a dream it's

thrown down and buried
in another man's chest.

He likes to picture himself
before his heart became sacred,

before he became the town wound
that wouldn't stop bleeding.

II.

Brides of Christ argue
in the chambers of his heart:
that little red house with the picket fence,
always on fire.

Heaven's a bed
in a smoke-damaged room:
women sleep at the edge
of the hole in Christ's chest,
hair tangling on ribs
and matting with blood.
Their halos smeared down
with blood on the light.

This is the house
with a gash for a door.
The Bridegroom lifts his lovers
over its threshold's ragged
edge of flesh.

III.

Through my fingers
the rosary's a tangle
I can't get out;
each prayer smashed
on its own cheap bead.

All my desire
trapped in one hand.

Someone untie me,
my heart that's restrained
by ropes of blood.

I'm the woman who laid down with Christ,
woke-up with a crime scene:
five doors left ajar in pools of blood,
lights on in the house,
no one answering my call.

Cathedral

There are rooms lit only
by flashcubes. In this one
lepers had their view forced
solely on the altar
through a slit.

For nave windows, no one slaughters
a cow anymore: light
filtered through the lining
of its stomach, a landscape

scraped of meat and blood.
This church took centuries to conceal
the Lord's torn body
in a chalice — the first soft parts
of the cathedral to go.

We're the last viscera in this place.
From the Lepers' Squint
I can't see you —
Is your ear against the wall
imagining the sound of my
hands disintegrating?

Once, even the smell
of windows drew wolves.

We've no need to identify
a speck as an army on the horizon
or a piece of meat
still clinging to the view.

Vellum (Ireland)

Look back too far
through Europe
and you're just another browser
in a library from slaughter: God's word
come down on backs of animals.
Monks scraping meat
off the page.

Where lie *my* more literate ancestors?
The ones thinking
that lamb was a book
to be butchered into being,
till nothing but paupers
wandered around in the fields,

scrounging potatoes —
Outside the walls
of smashed cathedrals,
my family's a field of hunger grass
risen to the top
of their unmarked grave. A lawn
my dead just don't want to rise beyond.

If heaven's the blue
ground out of a stone
and backed on an animal's hide,
my ancestors
imported the sky
all the way from Afghanistan
just to hand it over
to the church.

Gray's the color
left to everyone else: nothing
but rain on the guy
separating a meal or book
out of his animal. A book
begun in the yard,
spattering him with blood.

PART TWO

Traditions of Bread and Violence

When knife first encountered bread
it was after breakfast
through a wall of stomach.

The man died hugging himself
that meal inside him more precious
than his money. Even today

the levels knives most mortally enter victims
are the levels my innocent family find most comfortable
for slicing and spreading at home —
when standing, it's at the stomach,
when sitting, at the heart.

On which side of the blade
are my lips, my throat?

Knife, let me slide
my tongue across your teeth
and kiss you.

Perhaps all you need
is a little love, like this bread
I salve with butter.

On Seeing the *Portrait of a Dead Child*
by Juan Soriano, 1938

Little one,
I breathe in the last breath
shred on your teeth,
hear your blood lie down
in the dark to rest. For you,

tonight,
Mexico City's displaced lake
falls back as tears,

your death drags a garden away
from its dirt —
flowers lying down
beside you to die.

You're one more table set with
a child: better angel
than the sorry Guardian
who failed you.

Prayer tangles the hands
clasped near your body —
I can almost hear the two
heartbearts that woman hordes
inside her. The smallest
throws a bone fence
around itself, a trellis its own pain
can climb.

What can I tell you?
Out in my world
an infant's a suitcase;
a child surrounded
by dollar bills, razor blades. A woman
explaining to police how
her baby's bones
turned to cocaine inside him.

Salvage

The murdered girl
couldn't stay in the ditch.
She began to accumulate

beneath the eaves of our house:
strands of hair, buttons, rags
of her blouse woven

into the birds' nests to support
their chicks. What desperation sets a detective
dismantling nests

looking for clues? This could be his daughter,
roughhoused in the yard
and him pulling twigs from her hair.

The closer the detective gets,
the smaller that killer becomes.
It will take tweezers

to find him: shreds, shards, skin, strands,
as the man comes apart like a saint
shattered into relics.

The Mother Next Door
to the Murderer's House

Some nights I wake, my body hides
blood on the sheet beneath me.
When my babies smile at me in their sleep,
I imagine a knife opening a second smile
on each throat. Who's not guilty
of needing to see more joy in their children?

My own kitchen's full of bored knives
in their rut orbit from drawer, to dish,
to sink, to drawer.
They have propped our hands up three times
a day, against hunger and despair, for years.
I owe them, pray
what offering I place to their left
will satisfy.

History

Was it out of memory or fear
how the twelve expressions of those children's faces
huddled tight to one side of my camera?
While the professional in me pried them loose,
made them cry over and over into that newspaper's
lock of light,

I admit, I never laid a hand on those kids.
The night of that fire I hid
my 3/4ths water beneath the scum and laundry
of my face and suit. I held my camera up: a handicap,
an artificial limb of recollection
for those burning kids to forgive.

Now, no matter how loose the bedsheets,
I feel history each night.
How once out West, prison was a blanket
a sheriff pegged down over criminals
for lack of bars.

My love no longer shares
my cell. As if on fire, I too have looked
for any water. It's only metal and good manners
balancing my hand on this spoon,
keeping me from washing my guilt off
even in my soup.

Crime

So white, this beachsand
where police dump the last caresses of chalk
drawn around murders. You chose a sprawl
then lie in it.

The only upright on the beach, I'm
suspect, potential victim, mourner watching

white overlap white beneath then around you
into aftermath of massacres moving as Jonestown:
everyone encircled in the loving
arms of family, friends.

Lean up. Let me see what was once
a full moon above us
broken down now to crescent scars
of my nails along your spine.

How in pieces everything seems to last longer.

Fire/The Love of Objects

Tough objects show sympathy
under great heat: their agitated
hearts soften
while we burn and scream.

We are pained by their natural reactions.

Once humanity snapped
whole gardens off the earth
into the arms of the sick and loved.

The fork's stump-hand
offers no bit of food.

The closed mouths of vases won't answer
water or *flowers* again.

Ashes

Mother's sank to the bottom
among murder weapons. A tidal wave
finally scattered her ashes,
heaved her three miles
into Crescent City, California.

Mother, this isn't the town
you wanted to live in forever.
When the water recedes
you're the high water mark
on a living room wall,
the grit in a kiss. Dad wishes

he'd burnt your heart separate,
taken it with him
to his grave.
He can't bear to think of it —
the dust of your heart
settling on another man's casket.
Who can carry you back

into the ocean?
Through sunbathers, beachcombers: always
a party at the edge of your grave.

Findings by Dissection

I look more the survivor
walking away from
this wreck

covered with blood and oil.
This blue whale's heart
the size of a smashed Volkswagen.

As the man who proved
a man could crawl
the whale's aorta like a trench,

I'm the size of a plastic surgeon
working an explosion
out of a woman's face. How many times

my heart would fit
this accident
pulled out of water

onto the dock
where couples park. Inside
there's little room to fuck

much less to make love.

Recognizing Little Tortures

I called out for this: what's hidden

deep in concoctions
of rice and vegetables: soft versions
of hard plants once shoved
beneath fingernails.

If I talk with my mouth full, tell me:

How will I know
history let off the leash
when I can't recognize
the dog? How can I take seriously

my party of a mouth?
The more I talk, the wilder
light strobes in
between my lips. From a distance

I could as easily be coaching
some Polish immigrant in English: *Good!*
Now — Let animals and humans die
together under the same verb.

Excavations:
The Pigs of Gadara/The Bones in a Wall

Nothing's as naked as pigs —

God moved demons like thoughts
from the possessed men
into the swine

of Gadara. To brush dust off that city
is to reheap the hill
where that herd jumped

into the sea. Their sudden intelligence
recognized the soles
of Christ's feet

receding on water above them.
Such evolution
hangs in an aura on bones. Look

as far off as Rhode Island — A pig
stripped under teeth
was buried in the wall of a house.

Only forensics convinced you
you hadn't found bones
of a child.

Recognition in Time of Evolution

The house hasn't been built
that doesn't have a doorstep: abandoned bills
keep me up all night, crying
to be fed. They threaten a romance
of candelit dinners for life. My throat's
a grave I can't fill up, this ink
a detour of meat from my bite.

Do words soak in? Are they something
a roach could break its leg on?
Somewhere an artist is driving nails
inches above his rug
exhibiting for spidery life.
Darwin, do that bedtime story —
shut us up with a gang of mice
growing into coachmen.
Make them stay that way.

PART THREE

Excitement, The Need for

Only the crops know they're surrounded
by teeth: these fields, falling
again and again
on my plate.

Air, twist yourself
into a roar. Carry off this sad house.
I won't drive it back here
on wheels.

In Europe, surveyors plot the border
of a newly declared country
down the center of a house.

Nothing but highway
bears down on my living room,
and it's still years out of sight.

No one imagines the potential
motel of my home,
of its Bible-empty rooms —
Where are the Gideons, their guide
to every nightstand in the world?

I live out of my suitcase
like I'm going somewhere.

Vertical City

What would we do
with our impatience?
30 seconds at the office,
40 seconds among apartments
waiting for elevators to open —
rooms on rope,
rooms without rest.

In the vertical city
there are banquets on top
of the tallest buildings.

There will never be gardens
or the footsteps of celebrities
above our ceilings. Only love drives us
to a fifth floor reached by stairs.

Only pain
lands on a roof, the hurt
flown in from miles away.

Demolitions I

One move
and the neighborhood
goes shrapnel, homes driven
beneath our skin

to kill us.
A woman turns at a shatter

accepting a window
into her body — What use
is her lover's breath

dried to that glass
inside her? Mouth on
my mouth, your breath

scatters over my face.
Hold me as though
I'm shot through with tame metals —
vaccinations,
earring stems — War

stares like a workman,
its desire screaming into me
from unfinished buildings.

Demolitions II

Who carved up this house over miles? Here

a clump of bedrooms. Later
the dining room,
kitchen. Don't believe *Diner*,

Motel — the man insisting he divined
the spot of exhaustion
between towns,

then covered it
with beds. He can't validate
this location

for the driver
asleep at the wheel,
whose car careens into a field

fifteen miles away.
Is this where we'll come
when we're coming apart? You,

bringing me roses
by brute force. Me,
gritting my teeth

on their stems. What doesn't look
like a wound
won't knit back together. Turn on

the tv: Hope is a bombing
or storm, then a living room regenerating
on the side of a house.

Demolitions III

Emotion breeds sloppiness. Rage
leaves half a living room dangling
from a house in shock.
Someone strong must insist, *Walls!*
throw off your views!

so the building goes fluid,
literally pours
to the ground. This mirage
should quench only itself.

It's not enough to know
whether the woman on the fifth floor
pulled her lover close
out of love or terror

before embracing him and home
to the tiniest particle. Darling,
you have to look up. I want to believe
only accidents happen

under those parts of the sky
dotted with tourists.
Tourists drop down where war's
in suspension. We can dance
beneath their planes.

Illegals

The village I could have
vacationed in
walked off Mexico's map. I find it
cramming itself into one
three-story house in Los Angeles.

In that home:
the men who assembled
my mother's smile. The bite she drowns
nightly in a glass of water.

Who gets up in America
just to sit down
to a box of jaws, a table full
of teeth? By November
those men are looking for bones
in our bakeries. But here
when flesh falls away
there's no sweetness. Here

who will be anything to them
but the hardest part
of a smile?

This town's too small
to be marked on our map.
It waits to get shipped back
over the border,

to its acres of marigolds.
In the yard: whole fields
forced down to a garden;
men up to their knees in flowers
for the dead.

Skeleton Tableau

I am setting up a death
I can deal with: three skeletons
barely an inch tall.
A trio of x-rays
dressed in doll clothes.

Each skull's formed
over the head of a pin — Now
the angels displaced have to dance
on pins sunk in a voodoo doll's neck,
a beetle's back,
a basted hem (Their wings brush my knees.)
No angel watches over

these skulls. In their little motel room,
two make love to the Mexican
radio station
pulled in by the metal in their heads.
Is the third one Death
or the adulterer's wife
who's walked into this bedroom?

A room furnished like any U.S.
motel room: tv, a bed.
A fragment of mirror radiates
one-tenth of the bad luck
for whoever broke it
to decorate this then nine more rooms.

Test

Behind the doctor's door
your shirt hangs on thin shoulders,
a wire question mark at the neck.

In a cornfield on our first vacation
we hung our clothes in the furthest acre,
then took turns
with our backs in the dirt.
I didn't want to count
the bones in your body, each one
waiting to be named by a med student.

There's a love that can't fit inside
the normal limits of the heart —
two ribs break to accommodate
this affection suffered only by saints.

You've no wound.
Still, the lab technician
lingers over your blood, keeps it
two weeks in a refrigerator filled
with blood and birthdates.

I want to stay awake tonight,
feel the soft parts of our bodies
muffle each bone. If I sleep,
you're already beneath my eyelids,
hands feeling for the way
back into this world.

Notes on Our Future Disinterment

Nail my heart to my ribcage.
Watch it bleed through my blouse
like a mortal wound.

You'd almost believe I'm living.

Now paste two photos
inside my head, so you can see
your face in my eyes again.

Help shake this rattle
out of my skull —
pennies from my eyelids,
the silver dollar from my tongue.

My dear, our arms are still arms.
Don't listen to our bones,
each one's demand to be called
by its Latin name.

Things could be worse.
We could be saints,
our skeletons in splinters
on a thousand burning foreheads
in a plague town. The cured hiding
these relics, not giving our bones
back for resurrection.

Leaving the Emergency Room

Where are the seven weepy little men
over each of us?

I was a storybook failure
kissing a man who wouldn't
wake up on a table that wouldn't

thaw down.
In the blunt romance
of medicine, doctors touched the heart

I had only figuratively
touched, that broke over something
having nothing to do

with myself. I am going home
tonight. I don't know
who will love the wife

of the recipient down the hall —
her husband
or the donor heart

heading towards his chest
on a pile of ice.
As the wife of that heart

I'll follow as far as his bed.
I will have to be introduced.

All Hallows

Tonight, your ghost could come back to me

wearing two gashes for eyes
in the bedsheet I pulled
over your face. When you died

your family had you
burnt beyond bones,
into something they'd sweep
out of the kitchen, wipe off a table.

I wanted to sleep in your ashes.

Once, I was a child
pulling a skeleton to my skin
and stepping into it.
Door to door I received

what only the dead
of All Hallow's receive:
a stranger's generosity,
a sweetness

pooled in the bottom of a sack.

Heaven

When the coroner laid
your heart on his scale,
Cupid was no more than a pest
buzzing over raw meat.
Sorrow put me at the tip of Chile,
sobbing uncontrollably
whether I stared at you
or a rock.
Drivers turned on their air conditioners,

opened the sky over us. In that hole,
the hand of God
was nowhere to be seen.
You lay down in your grave
facing east
only by chance. Even here,

In God We Trust
is the tiny message
I'm forced to desire in handfuls
whether I believe in Him or not.

Opening the Border

Stand on it long enough

and a bridge appears
in a town with no river.
An entire state's flowers
wilt in the fields.

Someone's drowning my lover
in cheap Mexican roses —
He washes ashore

at a shrine: Let me choose my support
from abandoned crutches, then pin
to the wall the shadow
of my heart,
ribs lifted as
light from my chest.

                    *   *   *   *

Here is my body: broken suitcase
closed with blood's long rope.

My heart is its dark knot —
Just try and untangle it from my
one dead love.
He's scent that follows me
over the border,
to this motel room. Over our bed:
the love of a heart
embellished with knives;
saints kept awake
by their own glowing heads;
the face that Mexico
hangs on heaven, nailed always
just out of reach:

Our Lady of Guadalupe —
a residue of roses
on cloth, woman
locked in an aura of thorns.

* * * *

Eight hours a day,
women make the same gesture
over and over. A movement
turning out only teeth,
masks, garage
door openers. Their children

beat on a star
dangled low enough to strike.

What am I doing here?
The dead aren't due back
for another six months,

every wish in Juárez
vies for the same, dull star
night after night.

I am one of the women who whisper
deep into the gash in Christ's side —
that second mouth leading
straight in.

* * * *

There was no calming
your terrified soul
beating itself to death
against bright white lights.

How long do I have to keep
peeling the sheet
off your cracked-open chest,

cutting my face on your ribs,
pressing my lips to your heart
to weep into your blood,
your body
laid out on a table
the color of knives —

On your doctor's wrist,
a bracelet of blood.

I keep signing the cross.
I can't sew my heart shut.

       *   *   *   *

Walk the highway
and here's how the dead appear
at the side of the road:
bouquet of marigolds,
a cross. A dazed soul left without
his car, his bottle, his
bullet, his knife — that last object of
his desire.

Trucks bear down on us
filled with flowers.

Love, let me lose you
in the smell of bone
rising from fields of flowers
for the dead, their acres of scent.

When We Absorb Sound

What use rubbing perfume, kisses
across wrists steeped in anger?
Blame physics, how

arguments came up
through the floor, the table legs and top
to enter my resting arms. Somewhere

screams travel miles
before finding a body
to absorb into. In this city,

one word, three feet from my lips
gets torn apart
by a crowd. What needle

can we press to ourselves
to play our thin history
back verbatim? Held, even you can't

relieve my wrists of voices
small as our neighbor's tensions.
Darling, let's say *I love you*

into each other again.
Here comes the soft part.
Relax.

There's no turning that music
off fast enough
to avoid being hit.

Catherine Sasanov was born in Rockford, Illinois. Over the years, she has traveled widely, including two years living in São Paulo, Brazil. She has received fellowships from the National Endowment for the Arts, Mexico's Fondo Nacional para la Cultura y las Artes (FONCA), and the Massachusetts Artists Foundation. In 1995, she was the recipient of an NEA Creative Artist's Residency in Mexico City. She currently lives in Cambridge, Massachusetts.

Poetry from Four Way Books

Brox, Orlowsky, Rhodes, editors *The Four Way Reader #1,*
    an anthology of poetry and short fiction

Lynn Domina *Corporal Works* (winner of the Four Way Books
    Intro Series selected by Stephen Dobyns)

Stuart Friebert *Funeral Pie* (co-winner of the Four Way Books
    Award Series selected by Heather McHugh)

Sarah Gorham *The Tension Zone* (co-winner of the Four Way
    Books Award Series selected by Heather McHugh)

Pamela Kircher *Whole Sky*

Stephen Knauth *Twenty Shadows*

D. Nurkse *Voices Over Water* (an Encore Series selection)

Catherine Sasanov *Traditions of Bread and Violence*
    (a Stahlecker Series selection)

Beth Stahlecker *Three Flights Up*
    (with an afterword by Ellen Bryant Voigt)

Sue Standing *Gravida* (winner of the Four Way Books Award
    Series selected by Robert Pinsky)

M. Wyrebek *Be Properly Scared* (winner of the Four Way
    Books Intro Series selected by Gregory Orr)

Four Way Books is the publishing arm of Friends of Writers, Inc., a Vermont-based not-for-profit organization dedicated to identifying and publishing writers at decisive stages of their careers.